199 ideas

Powerful Marketing Tactics That Sell

BY SHERI JACOBS, CAE

PUBLISHED BY

ASAE & THE CENTER FOR ASSOCIATION LEADERSHIP

asae & the center
for association leadership

WASHINGTON, D.C.

The author has worked diligently to ensure that all information in this book is accurate as of the time of publication and consistent with standards of good practice in the general management community. As research and practice advance, however, standards may change. For this reason it is recommended that readers evaluate the applicability of any recommendations in light of particular situations and changing standards.

ASAE & The Center for Association Leadership
1575 I Street, NW
Washington, DC 20005-1103
Phone: (202) 626-2723; (888) 950-2723 outside the metropolitan Washington, DC area
Fax: (202) 220-6439
Email: books@asaecenter.org
We connect great ideas and great people to inspire leadership and achievement in the association community.

Keith C. Skillman, CAE, Vice President, Publications, ASAE & The Center for Association Leadership
Baron Williams, CAE, Director of Book Publishing, ASAE & The Center for Association Leadership

Cover design by Beth Lower, Art Director, ASAE & The Center for Association Leadership
Interior design by Troy Scott Parker, Cimarron Design

This book is available at a special discount when ordered in bulk quantities. For information, contact the ASAE Member Service Center at (202) 371-0940.

A complete catalog of titles is available on the ASAE & The Center for Association Leadership website at www.asaecenter.org/bookstore.

ISBN-13: 978-0-88034-319-0
ISBN-10: 0-88034-319-2

Printed in the United States of America.

10 9 8 7 6 5 4 3 2 1

CONTENTS

INTRODUCTION

Howard Gossage, a well-known adman from the 1950s and 1960s once said, "People don't read ads. They read what interests them and sometimes that happens to be an ad." Although he made this statement decades ago, it is as true today as it was back then.

People rarely notice advertisements (in any form) unless one or more of the following conditions exist.

– The message is highly relevant to them at the moment they receive it.

– The message is both highly memorable *and* unique.

– The message touches an emotional chord.

So, how do you write marketing copy that will sell the things your association offers, both tangible and intangible?

You must know *everything* you can about:

1. What you are selling.

2. Who you are selling to.

3. Your competition.

4. The psychological or subconscious factors that influence a decision.

5. How you want the prospect to act.

KNOW EVERYTHING YOU CAN ABOUT **WHAT** YOU ARE SELLING

1. Conduct an asset audit.

To better understand what you are selling and who it may appeal to, conduct an audit of all of your assets. For example, if you wish to attract younger members to your organization it is essential that you are able to identify programs, products and services that are affordable and of high interest to this audience segment. Simply promoting all of your organization's assets will dilute the message.

An association's assets typically include publications, educational programs, web content, networking events, volunteer opportunities, and other tangible offerings. Once you've listed all of your organization's assets, complete a chart by answering the following questions for each item.

- Who (member type and career stage) is interested in your program, product, or service?
- Is the offering something that can be easily referred to others? If so, rate it on a scale of 1–10, 10 = high likelihood to be referred.
- Does it use technology to deliver its value?
- Is it tangible or measurable?
- Is it expensive, moderately priced, inexpensive, or free?

	Associations Now (Print)	Technology Conference	Annual Conference	Models and Samples	Membership Listserv
Audience(s) served	All levels	CEOs, Senior Staff	All levels	All levels	Membership professionals
Referral rating (10=high)	10	1	1	10	10
Uses technology to deliver	No	No	No	Yes	Yes
Tangible or measurable	Yes	Yes	Yes	Yes	Yes
Less than $500	Yes	No	No	Yes	Yes
Less than $150	Yes	No	No	Yes	Yes
Less than $50	Yes	No	No	Yes	Yes
Free with membership	Yes	No	No	Yes	Yes

Source: Sladek, 2006.

2. Define Your Unique Value Proposition (UVP).

Clearly define the features, advantages, motives, and benefits of what your organization offers by conducting a Benefit Analysis.

- Features describe the actual program, product, or service. In most cases, the features are the physical or tangible characteristics that describe your offering.
- Advantages distinguish the feature as unique or special.

- Motives describe what the features satisfy as a result of buying and using your "product."
- Benefits are the favorable or desirable experience the buyer will have as a result of purchasing your offering.
- Evidence is found through program evaluations, surveys, and buyer feedback.

Feature	"How to Write Marketing Copy that Sells" half-day workshop
Advantage	Learn from one of the top association marketer's in the industry. Find out what time-tested strategies, tactics, and techniques helped her increase membership at her association by more than 30 percent and attendance at her annual meeting by 60 percent.
Motive	1. Your job requires you to write the marketing copy to sell membership, meetings, or other products and you don't have a copywriting or marketing background. 2. Your efforts to boost response rates to your recruitment campaign have fallen short of your goals. You need to know what works.

Benefit	1. You will significantly increase your ability to sell anything.
	2. You will discover how to sell intangible benefits, such as advocacy or networking.
	3. You will understand how to use emotion and logic to:
	   – Increase attendance at your next meeting.
	   – Increase membership.

Evidence	1. 98 percent of past attendees rate this course as the best copy writing course they've ever taken.
	2. Sheri Jacobs, CAE,
	   – received a 4.7 out of 5 and
	   – was the highest rated speaker at the Marketing & Membership Conference.

3. Identify at least one differentiating factor.

Determine what is unique about what you are selling. You only need one factor that is different from your competitors. The differentiating factor could be your organization's reputation, the depth and breadth of your offering, the network connections membership offers, the price value equation, or 24/7 access to all of the information your members need with the click of a mouse. If you don't know what differentiates your offering, conduct a competitor's analysis. (For more information, see Tip 18.)

4. Interview the product manager.

Sit down with the staff person who manages the product you need to market and have an in-depth discussion about it. For example, if you need to write copy to sell an educational program, find out everything you can about the program, the audience, the content, the learning objectives, the speaker, logistics, and recent program evaluations if the program was available in the past.

5. Use a creative brief to define your objectives, tactics, and outcomes.

A well-constructed creative brief clearly defines the framework of a project for both the creative team and your colleagues in other departments. A creative brief will ensure everyone is on the same page in regards to the nature of the product and what is expected from the marketing copy.

Creative Brief

- Brief description of product or service
- Role of product or service. (By using the product, what will the end user receive?)
- Target Audiences. (Who will be most interested in this product or service?)
- Past marketing efforts and results. This includes a brief description of tactics used in the past and their return on investment (ROI).
- Competitors. (A list of competitors and how their specific products compare—including market share)
- Primary message. What is the single most important message the audience should recall after seeing the marketing?
- Supporting Statements
- Budget
- Success Measurements
- Timing

KNOW EVERYTHING YOU CAN ABOUT **WHO** YOU ARE SELLING TO

6. Find out what motivates your members and prospects.
Understanding what motivates a buyer to make a purchase is an essential element in being able to write effective marketing copy. Consider these questions. Do you know why members join, register, or make a purchase? Do you know the specific issues they are facing at the time when they make the decision to purchase? Do you know what they need based on their size, location, business, or other demographic factors? Do you know what keeps them up at night? If you don't know the answers to these questions, find out.

- Review inquiries to your customer or member relations department.
- Conduct a member needs assessment.
- Ask new members via telephone or email within the first 30 days of their membership why they joined your organization.

7. Find out what nonmembers think.

Focus groups, telephone interviews, and surveys are useful when you want to hear from members, however it can be extremely challenging to engage nonmembers in a conversation about their challenges, needs, and interests. Without an existing relationship, many nonmembers ignore invitations to participate in an association-sponsored research initiative. If you have trouble collecting information from this group, try "man-on-the-street" interviews.

To conduct "man-on-the-street" interviews find an event where a significant number of nonmembers will be in attendance. If another organization offers the best opportunity to meet nonmembers, ask permission to interview attendees at their annual meeting expo. Next, create and print 20–30 copies of a brief interview guide and attach the copies to a clipboard. The guide should consist of 5–7 multiple-choice plus demographic questions (gender, age, practice area, etc.). An example of a multiple-choice question you could use is:

"Why haven't you joined XYZ association?"
- ☐ I was unaware of the organization.
- ☐ No one asked me to join.
- ☐ I am a member of _____ organization and I feel that they serve my needs.
- ☐ The price is too high.
- ☐ I was a member and I let my membership lapse.
- ☐ I disagree with _____.
- ☐ Other _____.

Bonus tip: Approach people who are standing in long lines such as registration or a book signing event. Individuals are more open to answer a few questions when they are stuck in line and need to pass the time.

8. Subscribe to industry blogs—and read them frequently.

Blogs offer some of the richest sources for unsolicited and anecdotal feedback on many of the important and relevant issues facing an industry. To find a list of blogs for your industry, go to Technorati.com. Technorati is a web-based search directory for blogs.

9. Create a social media profile of your members.

Survey your members to learn where and how they spend time online. Organizations frequently select the technology or social networking tools before determining where the people are and how they are behaving. To avoid this mistake, conduct a simple survey of your members. Ask members how frequently they do the following activities (more than once a month, less than once a month, or not at all) (Li and Bernoff, 2008).

- Read reviews on Amazon, Yelp, or Epinions.
- Write reviews on Amazon, Yelp, or Epinions.
- Publish or maintain a blog.
- Comment on someone else's blog.
- Read a blog.
- Watch videos created by others on websites such as YouTube.
- Post videos to websites such as YouTube.
- Read online forums or discussion groups.
- Post questions to online forums.
- Respond to questions posted to online forums.
- Visit Facebook.
- Visit LinkedIn.
- Update a Facebook profile.
- Update a LinkedIn profile.
- Add comments to someone's page on a social networking site.
- Post ratings/reviews of products or services on sites such as Amazon.
- Listen to podcasts.
- Use social bookmarking sites such as del.ici.ous or StumbleUpon to tag content.

- Manage RSS feeds using an aggregator, such as feedburner, google reader, or newsgator.
- Add tags to web pages or online photos such as on Facebook.
- Write articles or stories and post them online.
- Post updates on Twitter.
- Retweet articles or other tweets.
- Follow others on Twitter.

10. Create an internal social media listening group.

Every department within an organization can benefit from having a constant stream of information regarding the key issues being discussed by members and prospects. A social media listening group collects and catalogs conversations and topics being discussed on blogs, Twitter, LinkedIn, Facebook (your association's fan page and pages set up independently of your organization), and other media outlets.

11. Identify your top influencers.

In every industry, a small group of individuals produce the majority of postings on social networks. Create a list of individuals who have a large number of followers to their Twitter account, blog, or Facebook page. Listen to what this group is saying about your organization, your industry, and your competitors. Incorporate their issues and challenges into your marketing copy.

12. Make it a practice to test, learn, and adjust your marketing copy.

Track the performance of all your marketing efforts. Sometimes it just takes changing one word in your marketing copy to get dramatically different results. Don't make the assumption that one type of marketing tactic is ineffective just because your campaign did not produce the results you expected. Test, learn, and test again. Plus, test only one element at a time for accurate results. The following are some variables you should test.
- Offer
- Word selection
- Images

- Placement of text
- PS statement
- From line
- Subject line
- Time/Day
- Deadline

13. Create ways for members to generate buzz.

Have you ever created a *Member-get-a-Member* campaign that did not produce the results you were looking for? There might have been a number of factors that contributed to this, however if you were looking to harness the power of word of mouth and create true buzz within your industry, you need to make sure at least one of the following factors exist.

- The topic being discussed is controversial or highly relevant.
- You offer something new, such as a new perspective, new content, or new information.
- You surprise your recipients by giving them something completely unexpected yet valuable.
- You offer a product that is of significantly higher quality than your competitors.
- You under promise and then over deliver.

14. Comment on news stories or research papers; track issues on Digg.com.

Turn your ad copy into newsworthy commentary. Identify hot issues in the news that are relevant to your organization and share your comments on the topic, even if they are controversial. Create a conversation about an issue and connect it to your organization, your programs, your products, and your services.

15. Connect your brand to an expert.

Conduct interviews with experts and post the copy from the interview on your website and in your publications (electronic and print). When potential buyers are searching for a term or a subject, your interview with an expert may appear on a higher page in Google than your organization's home page.

16. Use contextual targeting to spread the word.

Contextual targeting is an extension of search advertising. A contextual advertising system scans the text on websites for keywords and then produces advertisements based on those findings. For associations, this provides an opportunity for their advertisements to appear only on highly relevant websites. The Google content network, one of the online advertising tools available for contextual targeting, reaches 80 percent of global internet users (Google AdWords). Google uses contextual targeting so that your ads appear on the most relevant websites, blogs, industry publications, and social networking sites.

KNOW EVERYTHING YOU CAN ABOUT YOUR COMPETITION

17. Identify and track your competition.

Associations compete with many different types of organizations for their members' time and money. Competition comes in the form of companies that offer continuing education (CE) credits, books and publications, or networking events. Competition can also come from local, state, or national associations as well as specialty associations. Create a list of competitors and update the list every quarter. Even if there are no changes, it is a good reminder of who else is competing with you for your members' and prospects' attention.

18. Conduct a competitor analysis at least once a year.

Identify the strengths and weaknesses of your competition. Monitor how they market their offerings. Look at the following factors.

- Location (meetings, educational programs).
- Pricing (a la carte/bundled).
- History (length of time in the marketplace).
- Products offered (depth of their portfolio).
- Brand (loyalty and awareness).
- Audience segments served, market share, growth rate.
- Promotional mix (budget, strategy, tactics, advertising theme, and tone).
- Pricing and discounts.

19. Put yourself in the shoes of your buyers.

Conduct a Google search to determine what ads appear when your buyers or members look up key words? How are other organizations promoting their offerings? Identify your competitive advantage as viewed from the buyer rather than from your perspective.

KNOW THE SUBCONSCIOUS MOTIVATIONS THAT WILL GET YOUR PROSPECTS TO BUY

20. Create a sense of a "good deal."

Value and price are both relative variables. A one-day educational seminar that costs $229 to attend may seem expensive at first glance to a buyer. If, however, you promote the regular fee as $299 and a special offer of $229, the buyer will believe they are receiving a "good deal" and will be more likely to register at the $229 rate.

No one wants to feel that they are paying too much for something. By comparing items with similar features but a higher price tag, you can create a sense that the buyer is receiving an exceptional value. This logic helps buyers justify their purchase.

21. Create a tone that matches your product.

The words you select to sell your programs, products, or even membership set a certain tone. While two words may have the same definition, their impact on the buyer may be completely different. In some instances, your choice might be obvious. Other times, you need to test the use of different words to determine which ones will elicit the highest response. For example, think about the word FREE. You can use COMPLIMENTARY, INCLUDED, GRATIS, or NO ADDITIONAL COST or even just use the word FREE. What is most effective? It depends on your audience and the tone of what you are selling. The word you select should be based on the emotion you wish to elicit.

22. Promote the emotional needs your product will solve rather than the specific features.

For example, you aren't selling membership; you're selling increased job opportunities, greater earning potential, enhanced credibility, and a competitive edge in a tough job market. When Northwestern University wanted to promote its graduate program the copy they selected for their advertisements that appeared at bus stops in downtown Chicago asked "Do you have room on your resume for an MBA from Northwestern?" This statement cut right to the heart of the emotional benefit of attending the school's graduate program. If you are unsure about the emotional needs of your members—find out.

23. Ask a question that your prospects will say "yes" to.

Does your budget limit the amount of continuing education (CE) needed to maintain your credential? Are you looking for creative and budget friendly ways to gain new clients? Are you trying to serve your clients (or patients) and build a profitable business? All of these questions will typically elicit a resounding YES. Use your differentiating factor to determine the nature of your question. For example, if the differentiating factor for your organization is that membership includes access to free online education, on-demand, you may want to begin your promotional copy with the question: Does your budget limit the amount of CE you need to maintain your credential?

24. Write a headline that will ensure the prospect will want to read more.

Headlines should be used to capture a buyer's undivided attention. It must pique their interest and give just enough information to ensure that the buyer will want to continue reading. Look at every single sentence you write in your marketing copy. Does each sentence or statement lead the reader down a path that will end with him or her taking the action you desire? Review your marketing materials to see if they accomplish this goal. Eliminate the sentences that pull the buyer away from the intended message and desired action.

25. Make your prospect the focus of everything you write.

Make a promise you can keep and tell the prospect what's in it for them. Review the copy that appears on your website or membership brochure. Do you focus on your organization or your prospect? Words that just describe your organization elicit the response "so what." Words that describe your prospect and their situation will pique the interest of your prospect.

26. Use an involvement or action device.

Involve your prospect in the promotion. Do you remember the Publishing Clearing House (PCH) Sweepstakes? To enter the sweepstakes you had to move stamps from one part of the mailing to the entry form. This technique was used because PCH wanted to keep the buyer's attention on the mailing. By asking prospects to complete this action, PCH engaged them in the sales process and increased the number of entries and magazine orders they received.

An association that is marketing an educational program could ask prospects to list three issues they will address when they return from the conference and then provide space within the brochure or mailing to list the issues. If you are selling membership, you could ask prospective members to tell you what is the biggest challenge they face at their organization, what year they hope to retire, or what they hope their next career move will be.

27. Be an authority or an expert.
People are skeptical. They don't believe advertisements or broad claims. Demonstrate your authority by listing your credentials.

28. Be specific.
Avoid using the words *top-notch* or *top-rated* to describe your educational programs. Use a specific and believable statistic instead. For example, if your educational programs received high marks, you could state, "95% of past attendees rate this conference as one of the most important moves in advancing their careers."

29. Make it easy for buyers to take action.
The alternative to including an involvement device is to make it easy to take action. Find ways to make it easy to join, easy to register, easy to share, and easy to contact you. With each question you create a barrier to the sale. Determine the bare minimum of information needed to complete a transaction and only ask for it on your forms. Review your processes behind joining, registering, and purchasing products from your association. Simplify the first step.

30. Tell an interesting story.
To capture a buyer's attention, engage them in a story they can relate to. Listen to what attendees say after they've attended your events. Assign a staff member to ask attendees if they found the session they just attended to be valuable. Capture their exact words. For example, I conducted a quick search of a few association websites and I found that nearly the same copy was being used to promote many of their education programs.

> "We provide educational programs presented by top-notch speakers discussing cutting-edge solutions to the challenges you face." (Does this sound familiar?)

Another way to demonstrate your organization provides high quality education is to state:

"Wisconsin Society of Widget Manufacturers offers educational programs that are worth getting up at 5 AM and driving half-way across the state to attend."

31. Increase your credibility.

Identify and link your organization to well-respected people or institutions. Instead of saying "Attendees include executives from major healthcare institutions," say "Attended by C-Suite executives from the Anderson Cancer Center, the Mayo Clinic, and Johns Hopkins Hospital."

32. Give a reason why.

Your marketing copy should answer the questions on the minds of your buyers. Why should I attend your meeting? Why should I join or renew? Why do I need to earn your credential? Why should I volunteer?

33. Create an unconditional satisfaction guarantee.

An unconditional satisfaction guarantee eliminates risk. The stronger your guarantee, the more confidence you will instill. For example, if you are selling membership, promise potential prospects that you will refund their money, no questions asked—until the very last day of their membership. Let them know that you are so confident that they will value membership in your association that you are willing to back up your promise with a powerful unconditional guarantee.

34. Use the words "How to" in your headline.

The words "How to" tell the reader that he or she will learn something tangible and measurable.

Old Headline (Actual Titles)	Revised Headline
Copywriting 101	How to Write Marketing Copy That Sells
Tactics for Avoiding Rehospitalizations	How to Avoid Losing Patients to Other Hospitals
Introduction to Taxonomy Development	How to Create, Maintain, and Adapt Your Own Taxonomy
Exceptional Customer Service Builds Business	How to Grow Your Business and Keep Clients Happy After the Sale

35. Stay away from long paragraphs.

Studies have shown that people don't read long paragraphs. Use bullets or numbered lists to promote the details of your offer. Include only two to three sentences per paragraph, unless you are telling a story.

36. Use a number in your copy.

Numbers create a sense that you are offering something both tangible and measurable. Some numbers, however, are more effective then others. For example, if your number ends in 5 or 0 it creates a feeling that it was manufactured. When you use a number such as 6, 7, or 9, it just feels more real. One of the most effective ways to use this technique is by adding a number to your title. For example, which title sounds more real?

"11 Steps to a Successful Virtual Conference"

or

"10 Steps to a Successful Virtual Conference"

37. Use the word "because."

If something seems too good to be true a buyer won't believe what you have to say. They will want to know why you are offering something at such a low price. People are skeptical; they don't believe they can get something for free. Give a reason why you are offering free membership, free education, free shipping, or a free white paper. Tell people what's in it for them *and* what's in it for you.

38. Use short, simple sentences.

A recent examination of Amazon Text Stats showed that highly read authors used short sentences and simple words to make their point. (Johnson, 2007) Look for opportunities to break up thoughts or long sentences into shorter statements.

39. Avoid using all capital letters or italics to highlight an entire sentence.

These formatting features should only be used to highlight one or two words. *All three techniques, when used for more than one word, make it difficult to read,* case in point.

40. Add the word "you" to your marketing copy.
The word "you" is one of the most important words to include in your marketing copy.

41. Repeat what you want the prospect to do.
Repeat what you want the prospect to know and do as a result of your promotion. If you want them to join your organization, purchase a book, or register for a meeting, say it at the beginning, middle, and end of your pitch. You can do this by adding a brief sentence to break up copy or add a graphic image that repeats the call to action.

42. Create a sense of urgency.
Tell prospects they need to act immediately if they want to receive a special price; give a penalty for not acting now. For example, your marketing copy could state that, "only the first 20 people who register will receive a white paper, a discounted price, or a seat at the table."

43. Write with emotion.
Find a member, a volunteer, or an expert who is passionate about what you are selling and have a conversation with that person. Ask them to describe the challenges they face with specific and real examples. After you've had the conversation, begin writing your marketing copy.

44. Provide the name of a real person to call or email for more information or to make a purchase.
People want to buy from a real person not from an organization. While this may not be practical for all e-commerce situations, consider testing an email or direct mail promotion with a specific contact name versus one with a generic "contact customer or member service." Provide the name, phone number, and email address of a designated staff person who is ready to answer questions and help make the transaction easy and efficient. Try to avoid using "info@avenuemgroup.com" instead use "Contact Sheri Jacobs at jacobs@avenuemgroup.com."

45. Lower the perceived price by offering installments.

Installments lower the perceived price without discounting the value. If your members are resistant to paying $599 to attend your educational conference, try offering it for three installments of $199. This technique works for membership as well as products and services.

46. Give prospects a logical reason to join, register, or buy.

People make decisions based on emotion and then justify their decision with logic. A great example of this point is the recent advertisement for BMW. The carmaker first appeals to a buyer's interest in a luxury vehicle by building a brand around the tagline, "The Ultimate Driving Machine." They rarely showcase the car's features; instead they go for an emotional reaction to owning a BMW. Recent ads, however, create a logical reason for choosing a BMW over other vehicles because of a no-cost maintenance plan and other perks that actually help make the vehicle a logical choice. For your association, logical reasons may include the opportunity to save money, save time, or have access to something unique and available for a limited time. (Just remember to be specific. Don't say "save money" instead say "save $50 or 50% for a limited time") (Sugarman, http://www.psychologicaltriggers.com/)

47. Promote an offer that is available for a "limited time."

This technique is often used for meeting registrations however it could be applied to membership, booth sales, sponsorship, and product sales. If you promote your offering via email, state that a special price is only available a limited time with a link to your website.

48. Promote an introductory price.

If you are marketing a new educational program, promote an introductory price for the first year of the conference. For example, promote a $99 introductory registration fee and announce a regular conference fee of $199. Be sure to alert prospects to both the special rate and the regular price.

49. Offer something exclusive with your promotion.

Tell prospects that if they join today they will receive an exclusive white paper, invitation to an event, or product offering that is for members-only. Include the words "exclusive or invitation-only" in your copy to draw attention to the added bonus buyers will receive if they respond to your promotion.

50. Set limits on what you are selling.

Tell buyers that there is a limited quantity of what you are selling. If you are selling to a vendor community, place a limit on the number of "Gold or Platinum" memberships. If you are selling a publication, mention that there are only 50 copies of the first edition signed by the author.

51. Collect payment after you've made the sale.

Simplify the process so that the buyers only need to submit payment and contact information. Collect payment information after the prospect has registered or joined. They will be less likely to drop out of the buying process if they feel they have already "completed the sale."

52. End your price with a "7" or a "9."

There is a psychological price point for selling membership dues. For example, more prospects will join for $149 then will join for $150. Avoid ending your price with 0. (Rossell, 2009)

53. Create a "no-risk" offer.

Remove any risk of joining your organization. Offer a 30-day or 60-day free trial of membership. To ensure the prospect has the chance to fully utilize the free trial, create an instant membership if they apply online. The free trial should provide the prospect with all of the benefits of membership including discounts on educational programs and products.

54. Offer prospects the ability to upgrade or add to their purchase.

Many companies try to up-sell or add-on to the sale with related products or services once the prospect has made the decision to buy. For example, at Staples.com, once you add your items to the cart you are directed to a web page with suggestions for additional items you may purchase such as paper, pens, or file folders. The reason many companies use this technique is because once you've made a purchasing decision there is a high likelihood that you agree to additional purchases if asked.

This could apply to membership, education, sponsorships, or even product sales. The offer should appear either at the end of the marketing copy or during the payment process. Offer buyers the opportunity to purchase a publication, book, or subscription to your journal at a special price once they've joined your organization or registered for a meeting.

55. Build a campaign around a metaphor.

If your recruitment campaign looks and feels too much like a "sales" pitch or an advertisement, change the tone by building the message around a survey or an invitation. For example, if you use a survey as your metaphor, ask questions that will lead the prospect to say "yes." Finish the survey with a statement that says if they answered yes to any of the above questions then they should join.

56. Be original.

Find the one thing you have to offer that is unique and build your entire campaign around this single issue. Don't clutter your message by trying to sell every feature you offer. This will dilute your message and erase any sense that what you have to offer is unique and original.

57. Don't ignore objections. Address them.

Ask yourself why someone would say "no" to your offer. Come up with legitimate answers to possible objections. For example, if cost is an issue, demonstrate how the value exceeds the cost or offer money-saving tips. If the issue is lack of time (to attend an in-person meeting) address the concerns your prospects may have about being away from the office. Show them how they will stay connected. If membership in a competing association is the primary reason a prospect is a customer but not a member, identify and address the unique differences. Include a comparison chart in your marketing materials.

58. Write something that will make people stop and think.

Just a few years ago, researchers reported that people were bombarded with more than 3,000 advertisements a day. Today, you may receive that many before you've finished your first cup of coffee in the morning. In most cases, you have a few seconds to capture someone's attention before they hit the delete button or toss your mailing into the trash. Don't just promote what you are selling, ask a question or engage them in something that will make them read further rather than hit delete or toss your mailing.

59. Add an immediate call to action to *all* marketing collateral.

The decision to join, renew, register, or buy does not always occur at the end of your sales pitch. Some buyers will be sold after a quick review of your marketing materials while others need to collect all available information, compare options, and discuss the decision with others before making a decision. Audit all of your marketing and communications collateral to ensure you provide buyers with a way to act now regardless of where they are in the process. Every page on your website should have a join today or register now button.

60. Personalize your communications.

Personalization of your marketing materials creates a sense of familiarity. Most buyers are more likely to open an envelope that says "Dear Sheri Jacobs" then "Dear Prospect." By some accounts, using personalization in your marketing efforts will increase your response rates by as much as 30 percent. Use variable data printing to personalize the name, organization, title, and area of practice.

61. Leave out the brochure.

Nothing screams "sales pitch" more than a glossy, four-color brochure. Next time you launch a membership recruitment campaign, leave out the brochure. Create an A/B split of your prospect list and include a brochure with a letter in the mailing to group A and send group B just the letter. (To truly test the effectiveness of the brochure, leave all other variables the same.) By leaving out the brochure, you will change your marketing effort from a "sales process" to a personal communication.

62. Tell prospects what will happen if they buy, register, or join.

Use your most powerful benefit (not feature) to demonstrate what happens after you make a purchase.

63. Tell prospects what will happen if they don't buy, register, or join.

Identify a problem that may not get solved if they don't act today. Although this is similar to tip 62, this approach focuses on the negative aspects of not taking action.

64. Use a P.S to remind the buyer of a special offer or gift they will receive if they respond.

When people open a letter, more than three fourths read the P.S. line first. (Jutkins, www.nmoa.org/articles/dmnews/Postscripts407_RJ.htm) If you have a valuable, meaningful, and relevant special offer, the P.S. is a good place to bring attention to it.

65. Emphasize your guarantee in the P.S.

Guarantees create a sense of trust or comfort with your organization. Because the P.S. is the first part of the letter that is typically read by a prospect (especially a first-time buyer or prospect), it will be critical that you establish a sense of confidence at the beginning of your pitch.

66. Repeat your key benefit in the P.S.

If you are using a segmentation strategy, the P.S. is the perfect place to mention your key benefit to each audience segment.

67. Repeat your limited time offer in the P.S.

The P.S. offers another opportunity to repeat the details of your limited time offer including the deadline, special price, and redemption code.

68. Provide contact information in the P.S.

Don't obscure your contact information in your direct mail letter. If you include it in the P.S., you increase the chance that your reader will act immediately.

69. Use curiosity to keep the prospect interested.

To pique someone's interest, cite a statistic or fact that may surprise your audience. For example, if you need to promote an educational program on how doctors are using social networking sites to share information about diagnoses, you could state:

> 115,000 physicians use Sermo.com, a social networking site to get answers. Do you?

In this session, you will learn why they visit, who visits, and how this has made a dramatic difference in how they practice.

70. Create numerous drafts.

The first draft should be an outpouring of emotion and thoughts. Don't try to edit while you are writing. After you've written a first draft, put it down and go back to it a few hours or a day later. You will find some powerful ideas come out in your writing if you allow them to flow freely.

71. The higher the price, the more you need to say.

While short, simple sentences typically outperform lengthy ones, the higher the fee, the more information you will need to give to justify the investment. The same is true for an investment of time. If you wish to increase the number of members who actively volunteer with your organization and it will require a significant commitment of time, your marketing copy must answer all the questions on your prospects mind. (Sugarman, 2007)

72. Pretend you are selling face-to-face.

Write down what you would say in the order you would say it if you had to sell your product in person. Consider how you would first approach the subject, describe what you are selling, answer objections, and make your final offer. Your marketing copy should follow a similar format.

73. Form follows function.

Over the years, I've seen many brochures and advertisements that were clever and attractive yet failed to recruit new members or attract meeting attendees. Don't overwhelm your prospects with a beautiful design but difficult to read promotion. Your message should be prominent and the focus of the promotion—not the design.

74. Use serif type in your ad copy.
A fancy font may help your copy stand out, yet many are very difficult to read. If you want to draw attention to a key benefit, put your copy in bold or increase the font size and use a serif font. Serif fonts are much easier to read by a margin of 5 to 1. (Sugarman, 2007)

75. Avoid clichés.
Avoid the urge to incorporate a platitude or cliché into your marketing copy. By it's very definition, clichés are trite or overused expressions or ideas. At the very least, they will make your marketing invisible.

76. Promote your credentials.
If you are the authoritative voice for your industry, prove it. Give specific examples of what you've accomplished. Credentials include endorsements, awards, recognition, or achievements. Credentials also may include a list of recognizable members (individuals or companies) who "endorse" your organization by the mere fact that they have paid their membership dues or sponsored your event.

77. Write in a conversational tone.
Listen to what your members and prospects are saying about your organization and incorporate their actual words (not well-crafted testimonials) into your marketing messages. Try this exercise.
Ask a colleague to describe a recent purchase they made that they absolutely loved. It could be a new restaurant, a camera, a car, a cell phone, or whatever first pops into their mind. What words do they use to describe it? Why do they love it? Do they describe some of the benefits? Now look at your membership brochure. Would your members use the words you've chosen to describe their experience as a member?

78. Ask new members for feedback.
Your newest members are often the ones who are most enthusiastic about their membership. The reason they joined is still fresh in

their memory and they are full of expectations regarding how their career or knowledge will be enhanced by your organization. Call 30 new members and have a conversation with them about why they joined and what they hope to get out of their membership. Ask for permission and then take verbatim notes. Incorporate their words into your new member recruitment efforts.

79. Member Comments must be believable.
If you include quotations or comments from members in your marketing collateral, make sure they are relevant, believable, and attributed to real people. Always include the name of the person who gave the testimonial. The only exception is if you use feedback collected from anonymous evaluations. In this situation, be sure to note when and where the feedback was collected.

80. Use active verbs in your marketing copy.
After you've finished your first draft, reread it and edit to change passive verbs to active verbs.

81. Fragmented sentences are ok.
Writing copy for advertisements is not the same as writing for a newspaper, magazine, or journal. It's ok to use sentence fragments in your marketing copy.

82. Give your reader a transition.
Help the reader move from one paragraph or statement to the next with words such as "Since" and "So" and "That's why." These words help guide the reader so that they move from one part of your marketing pitch to the next.

83. Never end a page with a period.
If you've created a direct mail letter that requires you to use the front and back of a piece of paper, end the first page with only part of a sentence. This will require the reader to turn the page to finish the thought. Make every sentence, including headlines, a cliff-hanger— so the reader has to read on. (Baier, 2002)

84. Test and change incentives.

There are many different ways to offer incentives. Sometimes a small prize for everyone outperforms a chance to win a very large prize. In other situations, offering 25 chances to win a $100 gift card outperforms the chance for one person to win $2,500. The best way to find out if one would increase the results of your next marketing campaign is to do an A/B split and test different offers.

85. Use a coupon.

Coupons signal that you will be offering something free or for a discount. It is a visual clue that will give prospects a reason to continue reading what you have to say. Use a coupon to help sell membership, education, books, and other services.

86. Follow up on your leads.

A single letter and brochure is not a campaign. A campaign is a sustained effort over time. If your direct mail campaign does not produce acceptable results with the first or second mailing, don't give up. Follow up with leads. Most people don't respond to an advertising pitch until the sixth or seventh time they've received it. (Dobkin, 2003)

87. Use a BRE in your direct mail campaign.

A self-addressed, stamped, return envelope or a business reply envelope (BRE) almost always increases a campaign's response rate. The same is true for a pre-filled online form. Invest in the technology needed to connect your prospect database with your website and pre-populate a personalized URL.

88. Remember RUDI when naming a new product.

There are four basic rules to naming a new program, product, or service. The name should be Recognizable, Unique, Descriptive, and Imaginative.

89. Restate your offer in your response piece.

Your response piece, both online and in print, should always include a brief mention of your offer. This is one of the last points in the sales process where a prospective buyer may change his mind.

By restating your offer, you are confirming the sale and helping the buyer justify their decision.

90. Spend more time on the offer and less time on the creative.
Next time you set out to create a new brochure to promote membership or an educational conference, devote an equal amount of time and energy on creating the perfect offer as you do to developing the creative.

91. Offer additional value instead of a discount.
Instead of discounting your membership or your education, offer something free when someone joins or registers. Highlight the value-added offer so that the buyer understands they are receiving something extra for the basic price.

92. Increase the price.
Sometimes just increasing the price of a product increases the perceived value. A high price naturally eliminates people who cannot afford the fee. While you may not want to do this for your membership, this tactic may help build prestige around a special conference or retreat.

93. Use subheads to break up the text.
People skim text looking for something that is relevant or important to them. Make it easy for them to read your copy by breaking up the text. Use subheadings throughout your copy. Subheads will ensure they see the major points you wish to make and read any relevant information.

94. Be positive.
When writing marketing copy, avoid words such as *-ish, hope, try,* and *perhaps.* Use direct words that make a powerful and positive statement. (Benchmark Email, 2009)

95. Keep your outer envelope blank.
An envelope with no writing has to be opened to see what's inside.

96. Include a "Johnson Box" on your direct mail letters.

A "Johnson Box" is a rectangular box at the top of your letter above the salutation. This simple box is the second most-read element in a direct mail letter (after the P.S.). Put your offer in the "Johnson Box" and it will catch the attention of the reader.

97. Don't bury the guarantee.

Make it a prominent part of your marketing copy.

98. Add a Q & A section to your marketing copy.

Question and Answer sections are like Cliff Notes. Readers have grown accustomed to thinking that most of their questions will be answered quickly and succinctly in a Q & A section. Add a Q & A section to every communication device sent to members or prospects from your organization.

99. Timing is everything.

Resend your mailing to prospects. One of the secrets to getting buyers to open, read, and respond to your promotion is to make sure your marketing materials arrive in their mail or inbox when they are most interested in what you are selling. How do you know when a prospect is interested or needs what you are selling? You don't. Therefore, mail a simple, inexpensive direct mail piece such as a postcard to your prospect list at least five times during a campaign.

100. Use the phrase, "Last Chance" or "Time is running out!"

It may sound corny but it works because it captures people's attention and tells them they need to read your mailing right now.

101. People read postcards.

Use a postcard to sell membership, products, or education. It doesn't require someone to open it in order to read the important information in it.

102. Compare your speaker to someone famous.

If you have an unknown speaker for a topic that you are trying to promote, compare it to something your audience will know. For example, if the keynote speaker is Harry Markopolos, an expert fraud inspector, tell your audience that Harry Markopolos is to the topic of fraud as Sanjay Gupta is to medicine.

103. Know and monitor all of your marketing touch points.
Touch points include every interaction between your organization and the prospect or member. Some of your marketing touch points include e-newsletters, email, public speaking, tradeshows, member or buyer service, forms and applications, social networks, websites, advertising, volunteers, and shared interest groups. Keep track of every touch point by audience segment. Constantly evaluate your distribution policy to ensure you don't exhaust the communication channels.

104. Exceed expectations.
Make a promise and then over deliver. When you exceed the expectations you promise in your marketing copy you generate organic word of mouth that spreads quicker than any campaign you could fabricate.

105. Cut your copy in half.
One good rule of thumb to follow after you've written your marketing copy is to cut your word count by 50 percent. (Smiciklas, 2008)

106. Add personality to your marketing copy.
People connect with people. Generic statements often appear contrived. Give real examples of real people using your association's offerings. Describe outcomes with real examples. Adding personality to your marketing copy will make it memorable.

SOCIAL MEDIA AND OTHER MARKETING IDEAS

107. Include your members in the marketing process with a crowdsourcing tool.

Crowdsourcing, by definition, means to take a task, typically conducted by an employee, and outsource it to a group or crowd of people in the form of an open call. (Wikipedia, www.wikipedia.com) Online crowdsourcing tools provide organizations with the opportunity to hear directly from their key audiences. Next time you need to name a program, product, or service, use a web-based tool such as Slinkset (www.slinkset.com) to engage your audience in the process. Slinkset is a custom social news site that may be used to create your own content and invite prospects and members to contribute or vote on a topic, program, or product.

108. Promote social sharing if you want your message to go viral.

Email is no longer the only way to quickly spread your message. With the explosion of activity on social networking sites, your word-of-mouth strategy should provide individuals with the ability to share content and information through social sharing tools. Social sharing tools provide readers with a simple and efficient way to share a link to your site (or reTweet what you are saying) via the dozens of social networking sites in use today. According to a Forrester Research study commissioned by ShareThis, direct personal channels amongst people have greater trust than public channels such as news alerts or RSS feeds; 70 percent of individuals trust messages they receive from someone they know through a social site. (ShareThis, 2008)

109. Create mobile marketing content based on behavior.

Find out where and how your members access your emails. If they access them from their mobile phone, use text rather than HTML. If you are creating emails to be read on a mobile phone, test the copy so that it can easily be read on the phone. Most importantly, make sure your members or prospects can easily respond to your email using their telephone keypad. Once someone opens and reads an email on their cell phone it is unlikely they will go back to that email when they return to their office. Sometimes you have only one chance to get people to respond or act.

110. Monitor the conversation with PR Newswire.

Use PR Newswire to monitor the conversation about your organization and your industry. The social media metrics tool allows you to listen to conversations, weed through the noise, identify the demographics of people who are discussing your organization, and know when a conversation is occurring.

111. Bring your copy to life with YouTube.

If a picture is worth a thousand words, a video is worth…well you get the picture. Create a video using real members or staff and put it on YouTube. Humor is one of the best ways to create a viral YouTube video. A talking head, such as your board chairperson or the executive director, tends not to go viral. Once you've created your video, link to it in your emails, and on your website.

112. Monitor your keywords.

Every three to six months, research what keywords are most applicable to what you are selling. Incorporating the right key words will help prospects find you when they conduct an online search. Use Google AdWords' keyword tool to identify the best words for your organization and website. The AdWords tool will show you the approximate number of searches conducted on Google for words and phrases that you enter, or for phrases associated with a URL of your choosing.

113. Place your keywords in the right places on your website.

Once you've identified your keywords and phrases, use them in the most importance place where search engines will consider them. The search engines give the content of the title tag the greatest weight of any single element on the page, so your most appropriate key phrases better be there. (Niles, 2009)

114. Develop and maintain a linking strategy for your website.

Link to other great content websites and ask them to link to your website. This can be accomplished through social media websites such as Facebook, Twitter, and LinkedIn.

Graphic Design Tips for Marketing

115. Use white space to draw attention to your copy.

Allow for lots of white space in your marketing piece. The more white space, the easier it is to read your copy.

116. Use graphics to repeat your point at a quick glance.

Identify content that can be easily converted into a graphic image. Examples of graphics include pie charts, tables, photographs, timelines, and cycles. All of these elements will be the first item the prospect will look at when they review your marketing piece.

Bulleted or numbered lists also provide a visual clue to what you are trying to sell.

117. Use color with restraint.
Only add color when it enhances your message or reinforces your organization's identity. The overuse of color prevents branding. A single color highlight on a page will provide significantly more emphasis then the use of multiple colors. (Parker, 2007)

118. Proof your work from a printed copy.
When you start proofing, begin with the last page and work forward. Ask colleagues or professional editors to proof your work. In most cases, you will think you see the words you intended to write. (Parker, 2007)

Generating Word-of-Mouth

119. Give them something to talk about.
To generate word of mouth you need to give your members and prospects something worth sharing. When I was at the Association Forum of Chicagoland, we gave members an education gift card when they renewed their membership. The gift cards were mailed to all renewing members once we received their dues payment. The gift card was similar to one from iTunes or Barnes and Noble. It was branded with the forum's logo and tagline and it had a scratch-off line with a unique code that could be applied to any half-day education program. Renewing members were so excited to receive the card they quickly told their colleagues about it and encouraged them to renew their membership. As a result, membership renewals came in at a record pace.

120. Ask for feedback not testimonials.
Testimonials almost always appear contrived or manufactured. Ask for honest feedback and tell members or customers that you wish to use their comments in a future promotion. You will receive copy that is believable and relatable to your prospective audience.

121. Avoid acronyms and technical jargon.
Although your members may be familiar with your acronyms, prospects or early careerists may feel disconnected if you use them.

122. Look at your competitors' ads and differentiate your ad copy.
Before you begin writing your next ad, take a look at what other organizations or competitors are saying in their advertisements or marketing materials. This will ensure you differentiate yourself in your promotional copy.

123. Photos speak louder than words.
Include images of real people in your marketing materials. Studies have shown an increase in interest if a photo of a person is present in the advertisement. (Graham, 2000)

124. Promote an educational program with content from a speaker.
Ask speakers from your educational programs to provide tips or key findings from their presentation that you can distribute to promote a conference.

Brochures

125. Apply the five-second rule to reading your brochure.
Brochures should focus on capturing a prospect's attention within a very short time-span. Test your brochure to see what someone can learn by reading it for only five seconds. If the reader needs more information, they should be directed to a website.

126. Design a brochure so that it can easily be skimmed.
Most people won't read brochures; they skim it. Design the brochure so that if someone just skimmed it, they could get the essentials. To accomplish this, break up your text and use headlines and subheadings. Graphics are another way to convey a message you need to get across.

Checklist for Your Brochure

- ☐ Strong headline that communicates the benefit
- ☐ A compelling story that captivates readers
- ☐ Specific information needed to make a purchase decision
- ☐ Graphics and photos that quickly help tell a story
- ☐ List of features
- ☐ Comparison charts with competitors
- ☐ Specific data to back up your claims
- ☐ Believable quotes in a conversational tone
- ☐ Call to action at the beginning and the end of the brochure
- ☐ Contact information with an easy way to make a purchase

127. Include a *call to action* with a *Save the Date* postcard.

People rarely, if ever, use a *Save the Date* postcard to actually save the date of your event or conference. Only use it if you can entice the prospect to keep the postcard or there is a call to action. For example, if you want the recipient to mark their calendar and save the date for an event that is more than two months away, create a special offer that will encourage your reader to act immediately or tack the postcard to their bulletin board. An immediate call to action on a *Save the Date* postcard could be an incredible price reduction if they register early. Another way to get prospects to hold on to the postcard is to tell them to bring the postcard to your event and exchange it for something valuable such as a drawing for the latest electronic gadget.

Direct Mail Tips

128. Write a story.

A narrative lead is one that captures the attention of the prospect and allows you to clearly communicate what you are selling. One of the most successful examples of this type of writing was used by the Dow Jones Company to sell the *Wall Street Journal*. Written by Martin Conroy, the letter begins by telling a story of two young men who graduated from the same college and had accepted jobs at the same manufacturing company. Twenty-five years later, one was a manager of a small department and the other became the president of the company. A headline in the letter offers readers an explanation about "what made the difference." The letter showcases the benefits of a subscription to the newspaper in terms that are meaningful to its target audience. It also includes specific examples of what you will receive if you subscribe. The offer includes two pricing options, highlighting how one option is a *better buy*. The letter, reportedly, was directly responsible for bringing in $1 billion in revenues to Dow Jones & Co. (Kemske, 1997)

129. Use a strong offer to lead your letter.
If you are offering prospects a three-month free trial with no obligation to join, use this for the lead in your direct mail letter. To encourage prospects to act immediately on this offer, make sure you emphasize the value of the free offer and deadline to take action.

130. Flatter your prospects.
Tell prospects they were selected to receive this special offer of membership or an invitation to attend your event because they have accomplished something or achieved something. Sometimes just stating that the invitation is exclusive or only being sent to a select few creates a feeling of importance.

131. Include free items with your sales pitch.
If you are trying to sell a meeting or event through an email campaign, offer something free along with your sales pitch. You could give free content, a free white paper by a presenter, free research, or a free trial membership.

132. Announce the benefit in your lead.
If your organization offers a credential that is seen as necessary or instrumental to obtaining a promotion or a new job, begin with a statement or a question that immediately points out the benefit. For example, "9 out of 10 hiring professionals state that a credential gives job applicants a significant edge over the competition."

133. Design your outer envelope with the gatekeeper in mind.

For example, most CEOs do not open their own mail. Therefore, including a teaser on the envelope may have the opposite of the intended effect. A teaser may tell the gatekeeper that the letter is an advertisement or a sales pitch and it may be discarded before the intended prospect ever reads it.

134. Make it personal with a handwritten note.

A handwritten note signifies that the content is personal and relevant. This increases the chances that your marketing pitch will be read by your prospect.

135. Use a response form.

There are many alternatives to a membership application. A response form could be:

- Urgent Reply Form
- RSVP Card
- Reservation Card
- Free Copy Claim Ticket
- Free Issue Order Card
- Free Trial Membership Order Form
- Private Offer Saving Certificate
- No-Risk Trial Certificate
- Professional Courtesy Voucher

Checklist for a Response Form

- ☐ Is the form easy to complete?
- ☐ Is the offer clear and simple?
- ☐ Does it include an involvement device such as a check box, tear-off stub, sticker, or token?
- ☐ Does it provide multiple ways to act?
- ☐ Does it include a deadline?
- ☐ Does it clearly state the price and special discounts?
- ☐ Does it have a code for tracking?

136. Use a magazine tip-in to recruit new members.

An association's journal or magazine is often its highest rated and most visible offering. In many instances, the publication is circulated to colleagues who are not members of the organization yet are good prospects. If your members work in an environment that employs nonmember prospects, such as a hospital or a large company, add a membership tip-in to every issue of your publication (One of the key tenets of successful marketing is making sure you are visible when the prospect is ready to buy.)

137. Recruit *mailbox members.*

Some members join an organization primarily to receive information and to stay current on changes occurring within their industry. These members, sometimes called *mailbox members* may never attend an education program or volunteer, yet they are an important part of an organization's member base. How do you attract this audience? By promoting your publication. Promote a subscription to your publication and access to members-only information on your website. Offer a free trial issue and create a subscription form that is similar to the ones you see dropping out of rack magazines.

Website Copy

138. Pick three words that describe your key benefit.

What three words best describe the key benefit to joining your organization or attending your meeting? For example, if you are offering low-cost webinars on-demand, your headline for your website could be. Affordable. Online. Anytime.

139. Use logos and well-known name brands to give your organization credibility.

If your membership includes a high percentage of members from Fortune 500 companies, major healthcare institutions, or high profile companies in your industry, promote this. Add logos and names from well-recognized organizations on your website to call attention to a statistic you wish to promote.

140. Trim the copy on your website.

Your website shouldn't read like a book or white paper. If you can't shorten the text, break it up by paragraphs and different pages. Alternatively, you could provide a white paper that is available for download. One caution, search engines must find meaningful phrases on your page to show up in search results.

141. Change multiple/complex words—to one simple word.

Change complicated or lengthy text to read more simply, such as:

- Provided that—If
- In order to—To
- The majority of—Most
- Accordingly—So
- Facilitate—Help
- Frequently—Often
- Commence—Start
- Nonetheless—But

142. Remove all commas from your copy.

When you remove commas you force yourself to write shorter sentences.

143. Choose descriptive or helpful words for your website.

Don't state that your educational programs feature top-notch speakers on cutting edge topics. Tell people why a speaker is highly qualified and worth hearing in specific terms.

144. Give your visitor a reason to click forward not back when they get to your homepage after a search.

The two questions at the forefront of a visitor's mind are: What's in it for me? and Where do I click? The answers to both of these questions should be easily found on your home page.

145. Write a killer subject line.

The subject is the most important part of the email. Spend time writing a meaningful one that will inspire your recipient to open and read more. Don't forget, the entire purpose of the headline or subject is to get the prospect to read the next line.

146. Use your most compelling benefit in your subject line.

Consider the most compelling reason to join, register, buy, or just read your email. Use that reason in your headline for your email.

147. Avoid certain words in your subject (but keep them in the body of the email).

If you are not confident that the recipient will recognize your email address, avoid subject lines with the following words (save them for other promotions):

- Free
- 50% off
- Call now
- Discount
- Act now
- Special promotion
- Satisfaction guaranteed
- Information you requested
- Subscribe

148. Highlight key information in the preview pane of your email.

Create an email promotion that will show most of the vital information in the preview pane. In 2009, statistics showed that 69 percent of office workers use the preview pane at work to scan their emails. At home, about 27 percent of users choose the preview pane option. (Gomez, 2009) Make sure your message is relevant and grabs the attention of the viewer. View your email in your preview pane before you send it.

149. Move the most important information to the top.

Keep keywords, dates, offers, or prices right at the beginning of the sentence. In some cases, even a subject line can get truncated in certain email services. Don't leave the most important point to the end of your email copy. (Gomez, 2009)

150. The shorter the email the more likely it will be read.

Email messages must be short, readable, and have a clear focus. Convey only two to three points in your message. (Jerz, 2008)

151. Use a simple font type in your email.

Stay away from fancy typefaces, bold, italics, and capitalization in an email. Not only do these formats shout "advertisement" they also make it difficult to read.

152. Avoid attachments to emails.

If possible, copy and paste relevant copy into your email and provide a link to a pdf file. Attachments typically take too long to download. (Jerz, 2008)

153. Clearly identify yourself in your emails.

If you are sending emails to prospects that do not know you, identify yourself completely. Add your name and contact information to the body of the email.

154. Test your email before you send it.

Send a copy of your email to yourself and your colleagues to make sure all links work. Test the email to see if it will arrive in your inbox and not a junk folder. Do this with every email you send to members, prospects, and customers.

155. Test different subject lines in an email campaign.

Sometimes changing just one word or a phrase or highlighting a different benefit will yield dramatically different results. I've seen one subject line outperform the other one by as much as 30 percent.

156. Test different days for the highest response rate.

For some organizations, Tuesdays and Thursdays are the best days to send an email campaign. Other organizations have found success with Fridays or even Saturdays. The best way to know what is best for your organization is to conduct a test.

157. Free content is viral.
Offer a link to something free if you want your email to be passed along. It generates sales leads, creates a great opportunity to expose your ideas to a broader audience, creates brand awareness, and helps build search engine ranking. (Note: If you require visitors to provide their contact information to receive the free content then it isn't really free!)

158. Include social sharing tools in your email.
The use of a link that prompts the reader to "forward to a friend" has significantly decreased as individuals are flocking to social networking sites to communicate with each other. People love to share useful information on their Twitter, LinkedIn, and Facebook accounts. Make it easy for them to spread the word about your organization by providing the tools. Use a "Share to Social" link rather than a "Forward to a Friend" link to increase your pass along rate.

159. High levels of trust and affinity result in increased sharing rates.
The level of trust and the strength of the affinity between you and the recipient increase the likelihood that your email will be shared with others. Build a list of supporters or fans who have a deep relationship with your organization.

160. Build a campaign around the most common reasons people share emails (as paraphrased from *Groundswell* by Charlene Li and Josh Bernoff).
Examples of some of the reasons people share emails include:

1. Self-interest. They will benefit from a discount or a reward if they share.
2. Altruism. Sharing makes them feel good.
3. Validation. Sharing makes them feel important, it feeds the ego.
4. Affinity. Sharing makes them feel part of a community.

161. Give instructions.

If your community is new to social sharing, explain how and why they should share the information. Walk members through the steps they need to take to share information with each other using all of the social media tools available. Conduct "How to" seminars both online and in-person to help members become more acquainted with the technology.

162. Make your email readable even when the images are disabled.

Many email services disable images, even from known or frequent email senders. Although your members may download the images, prospects will be less likely to do so. Review your email as it may be read without any images. Is it still easy to read?

163. Track what is being shared—and by whom.

Once you've incorporated social sharing into your marketing efforts, track who is sharing, what they are sharing, and where they are sharing the information. These individuals are your organization's key influencers and should be included as a key component in your next marketing campaign.

164. Articles and statistics are typically the most share-worthy content.

Provide content, statistics, or information that is highly unique and timely and relevant to your audience.

165. Ask to be added to an address book.

One way to avoid having your emails end up in a spam folder is to ask your prospects, members, and subscribers to add you to their address book.

166. Create a "from" line that complements your "subject" line.

Readers will see the subject line and the "from" line at the same time, so there is no need to repeat the name of your organization in the subject line. (Lyris HQ) SmartBrief, a media company that publishes industry and best practice newsletters uses the "from" line to show the name of the newsletter and the subject line to capture a recipient's attention. For example, an email newsletter published by SmartBrief on social media uses a "from" line of *SmartBrief on Social Media* and a provocative subject line taken from one of the stories in the newsletter.

167. Brand your e-newsletter with the "from" line.
One way to avoid the junk folder is to create a brand name of your e-newsletter and use it for the "from" line.

168. Ask provocative or controversial questions.
If your members had a lively discussion on your listserv or your blog, continue the conversation in your email newsletter, your print publications, and your website. You can also start a discussion by asking a provocative or controversial question in your e-newsletter.

169. Use a reader poll to generate interest on a topic.
Including a reader poll in your e-newsletter provides a way to interact with prospects or members. It gives you some insight into attitudes and preferences. After you've asked the question, incorporate the response into a future email.

Other Tactics

170. Build a fan base not a customer base.
Are your members fans or customers? Fans are less price-sensitive and fully engaged. Fans tell other people (prospects) how much they love you. Fans will stick with you when there is a downturn in the economy. Their attachment is emotional. One of the best ways to build a fan base is to provide exceptional customer service that is truly personalized based on the needs of each individual member.

171. Ask Why at Least Three Times.
To get to the emotional reason or the true benefit of joining, registering, or making a purchase, ask the question why at least three times.

* **Why did you join ASAE & The Center?**
  "To meet and learn from other people in the same field."

- **Why do you want to meet other association executives?**
  "Because most people don't really understand what I do for a living."

- **Why is it important to be connected to other people who "get" what you do for a living?**
  - "Because they can relate to the challenges I face when dealing with volunteers."
  - "Because I can learn things from other association CEOs that I can't learn anywhere else."
  - "Because I don't have a colleague I can turn to in my office who understands or can provide advice when I need it."

Create a marketing campaign around the last answer to the question "Why?"

172. Be authentic. Show your personality.

People are drawn to real people, not brands, companies, or organizations. Forget the talking points and encourage your volunteers and staff to speak with authenticity. Don't filter their comments.

173. Give away 200 memberships.

Select something your organization offers and announce that it will be given away for free for an introductory period of time. What if you gave away 200 memberships every year? Or, you could give one free registration to every tenth person who signs up for an educational program through your website.

174. Offer something completely unexpected yet valued.

Imagine if you gave your top-selling book away for free. What would happen? You will obviously lose some revenue from book sales. You may also gain a stronger fan base that will stick with you and respond to other sales pitches.

175. Recognize your fans in print, online, and in-person.

Increase their visibility and watch others jump at the chance to join the ranks.

176. Reward your fans.

People become fans because they love a product or have an extraordinary experience. They stay fans when that reason is reinforced by future interactions. Reward your fans with something of value that is also unique or unavailable to the general population.

177. Create a group for fans on various social networking sites.
The fan group is different from your "regular" Facebook or LinkedIn groups. You must receive an invitation from another member to join a fan club. Fan clubs can be created around an event, an audience segment, or other criteria.

178. Give prospects a way to use what they purchase immediately.
People are more likely to purchase something if they can have it the minute they buy it. Create a way to give an instant membership, including digital versions of your new member kit.

179. Create a Squidoo Lens.
Squidoo's website claims it has "Google juice." Google loves Squidoo and indexes Squidoo lenses quickly. So what is Squidoo? It is a publishing platform that is fast, easy to use, and free. Lenses are pages, similar to flyers, where you can post short summaries on every topic and link the summaries to your organization's website. You can use a Squidoo lens for a topic or for an event.

180. Host free online events.
Invite all members, new and seasoned, to attend and make sure you tell them something new. Surprise them with a Starbucks gift card after they've registered for the event so that they can enjoy a beverage or treat during the event.

181. Ask your experienced leaders to market your organization by attending young professional events.
Volunteer leaders understand the value of your organization in real, tangible, and sometimes even measurable ways. They often tell stories about how they found their first position through a job posting or a connection they met at an association meeting. Invite your volunteer leaders to your young professional events and promote their attendance. They provide the bridge many young

professionals need to help them move from their current position to the next one.

182. Create a new member kit that reflects your audience.

Forget the pocket folder. Think about where your members work and how they would store and retrieve your membership collateral. If your members are office workers, send them a file folder branded with your logo.

183. Create a forum (online and in print) that is open to controversy.

Give members an opportunity to speak openly about their concerns, challenges, and viewpoints on subjects that may be controversial. You don't need to choose a side, just offer the place for the conversation to take place.

184. Increase your visibility when your competitors are pulling back their marketing efforts.

Increase spending during a recession. Your promotions will stand out even more in the marketplace.

185. Use the three Ws and one H to promote your organization.

Always tell people: What you do. What you get. What it costs. And How you compare.

186. "Join the 10,000 industry professionals who are members."

There is comfort in knowing you are joining a group that is considered the gold standard in the industry. Highlight your industry's endorsement by promoting how many members have already made the decision to join your organization.

187. Promote what is "included."

Tell prospective members that everything is included for one low price. Itemize the list of included features such as your publications, online resources, webinars and the membership directory.

188. Ask a new group of members every month "Why did you join or renew?"

Create a member panel and invite a small group of members to join and share their feedback. Stay on top of what your competitive advantage is from the members' perspective.

189. Use Repositioning Post-it™ Notes (RPN).

No one can resist reading a yellow Post-it note when it is attached to a postcard, direct mail envelope, or advertisement. It signifies that the message is important and worth reading and saving. Use RPNs to remind potential buyers about an upcoming deadline for registration, who to contact, or a special offer if they act immediately.

Attracting the Next Generation of Members

190. Use direct mail to reach Gen X and Gen Y.

According to the U.S. Postal Service, just over three quarters of Gen X-ers and nearly 80 percent of Gen Y-ers read direct-mail advertising. Plus, younger consumers rate 75 percent of the mail they receive as valuable.

192. Lower the price to attract early careerists.

Young professionals face a unique conundrum. How can they obtain the information and networking opportunities they need to advance in their career when they do not have the time to attend conferences or volunteer; nor have most reached the financial status of their older brethren, the baby boomer generation. Assess your association's portfolio and identify or create low-cost and technology-driven offerings that will appeal to young professionals. Promote these offerings specifically to this group.

193. Provide online peer-reviews about your programs, products, and services.

Gen Y-ers frequently turn to their peers for advice and recommendations. Engage current members and attendees in a peer review process and use the reviews to promote your offerings.

194. Create a sense of ownership.

Young professionals want to be respected and listened to. They want a seat at the table and they want their voices heard. Involve them in the development of your programs, products, and services and they will become exponentially more loyal to your organization.

195. Use contests to attract Gen Y.

Members of Gen Y have shown to be extremely enthusiastic about winning free stuff and entering contests. Whether it is a YouTube video contest or a free drawing, this generation is more likely to respond to this type of tactic than any other generation.

196. Demonstrate your diversity.

Gen Y is a diverse group of individuals. By some estimates, about one-third are minorities, primarily African-American and Hispanic. They have grown up in an environment that embraces and accepts differences in lifestyles and backgrounds. (Krotz, *Tough Customers*). At the same time, they are looking for a community that displays similar values. Promote your values and your diversity to attract members from this generation.

197. Use metaphors to explain what you do.

One of the best ways to explain what you do to a new audience, such as early careerists, is to create a metaphor. For example, *xyz* association is "Facebook meets Harvard." Come up with a list of possible metaphors and test them with staff, volunteers, members, and customers.

198. Display confidence.

Your marketing materials should reflect a strong and passionate belief in what you are selling. People are attracted to confidence. Display your confidence and your passion.

199. Promote just one thing.

Once you've determined what your members value based on their audience segment, select the number one benefit your organization offers and promote that singular benefit. Forget the laundry list of features. Just promote one thing; one unique benefit. Create a very strong link between your organization and that one benefit.

WORKS CITED

Arbabi, H. (2006, 17-April). From www.morebusiness.com/running_your_business/marketing/Isnare-17566.brc.

Baier, D. (2002). From www.wordbiz.com/archive/donnabaerstein.shtml.

Benchmark Email. (2009, August). From www.benchmarkemail.com/blogs/detail/writing-compelling-email-marketing-copy.

Dobkin, J. (2003). *Uncommon Marketing Techniques.* Danielle Adams Publishing Co.

Gomez, R. (2009, September). Email Subject Line Tips: How to Work With Preview Panes. From www.articlesbase.com/business-articles/email-subject-line-tips-how-to-work-with-preview-panes-1252541.html.

Google AdWords. (n.d.). From www.google.com/adwords/contentnetwork.

Graham, J. (2000). ClickZ. From ClickZ: www.clickz.com/831051.

Horn, S. (2006). *POP! Stand Out in any Crowd.* Perigree Trade.

Jerz, D. (2008). Retrieved 2009 from Jerz Literacy Weblog: www.jerz.setonhill.edu/writing/e-text/e-mail.htm.

Johnson, S. B. (2007, 21-October). Stevenberlingjohnson.com. Retrieved 2009, 8-October from www.stevenberlinjohnson.com.

Jutkins, R. (n.d.). National Mail Order Association. Retrieved from www.nmoa.org/articles/dmnews/Postscripts407_RJ.htm.

Kemske, D. B. (1997). *Write on Target.* NTC Business Books.

Khan, A. (2009, 30-September). AdwordsBuzz.com. Retrieved 2009, 30-September from Adwords Buzz: www.adwordsbuzz.com/2009/09/developing-your-content-creation-strategy.html.

Krotz, J. (n.d.). Tough Customers: How to reach Gen Y. From Microsoft Small Business Center: www.microsoft.com/smallbusiness/resources/marketing/small-business-market-research.aspx #ToughCustomersHowToReachGenY.

Levison, I. (2009). 101 Ways to Double Your Response Rates! Retrieved from www.levison.com.

Li, C. a. (2008). *Groundswell: Winning in a World Transformed by Social Technologies.* Harvard Business School Press.

Lyris HQ. (n.d.). Lyris. From Email Subject Lines: 15 Rules to Write them Right: www.lyris.com/resources/email-marketing/subject-lines/.

Niles, R. (2009, May). Top 10 search engine optimization tips for online news start-ups. From OJR: The Online Journalism Review: www.ojr.org/ojr/people/robert/200905/1733/.

Parker, R. C. (2007). Design to Sell Online. From www.designtosellonline.com.

Rossell, T. (2009). Membership Marketing Blog. From www.membershipmarketing.blogspot.com/2009/01/eight-tips-for-successful-membership.html.

ShareThis. (2008). From www.sharethis.com/about/press/4/.

Sherpa, M. (2007). Marketing Sherpa. From www.marketingsherpa.com/article.php?ident=29872.

Silverpop. (2009). From Silverpop: www.silverpop.com/downloads/white-papers/Silverpop-Engage-S2S-Study.pdf.

Sladek, S. (2006). *The New Recruit.* Expert.

Smiciklas, M. (2008). The Small Picture: A Visual Guide to Marketing & Management Ideas for Small Business. From www.intersectionconsulting.com/file/eBook%20-%20The%20SMALL%20Picture(1).pdf.

Sugarman, J. (n.d.). From Psychological Triggers www.psychologicaltriggers.com.

Sugarman, J. (2007). *The Adweek Copywriting Handbook.* Wiley.

Wikipedia. (n.d.). *Wiki.* From www.wikipedia.com.

ABOUT THE AUTHOR

 **Sheri Jacobs, CAE,** is the president and chief strategist at the Avenue M Group, LLC. She formed the Avenue M Group to provide associations with a smart, creative, passionate and experienced advisor around issues of marketing and membership.

A senior executive and an association management veteran, Sheri's marketing and association experience spans nearly two decades and includes roles as the chief marketing officer at the Association Forum of Chicagoland and director of membership marketing at the American Bar Association Law Practice Management Section and the American Academy of Implant Dentistry.

Sheri is a frequent speaker and a contributor to various associations and publications. She is a past chair for ASAE and The Center for Association Leadership Membership Council and a member of the 2009/2010 ASAE Marketing Council. She is also the co-editor and contributor of ASAE and The Center's official membership handbook, Membership Essentials. Sheri earned her BA in journalism and history from Indiana University.

For more information about Sheri Jacobs and her work with associations, visit www.avenuemgroup.com.

SHARE TIPS WITH COLLEAGUES

In our ongoing effort to connect great ideas and great people, we're collecting tips and ideas on a variety of topics that will be reviewed, and *if selected,* will be published in a future publication—a collection of "199" tips on a particular topic. You can choose to be credited as a contributor and if your tip is published be listed in the book as such, or you can choose to remain anonymous. Either way, it's a chance to give back to your profession and help others achieve greater success.

If you have questions about our "199 Ideas" series, please contact the director of book publishing at books@asaecenter.org.

Following is the submission form. We prefer that you visit www.asaecenter.org/sharemytip to submit your tip electronically via our website. However, if you prefer, you may copy and submit the form by mail or fax to:

Attn: Director of Book Publishing
ASAE & The Center for Association Leadership
1575 I Street, NW
Washington, DC 20005-1103
Fax: (202) 220-6439

Share My Tip Form

Please select the appropriate category or categories for your tip submission:

Board & Volunteers
- ☐ Board Relations
- ☐ Volunteer Relations
- ☐ Volunteer Recruitment
- ☐ Volunteer Engagement
- ☐ Volunteer Retention/Rewarding

Meetings
- ☐ Sponsorships
- ☐ Connecting Attendees
- ☐ Exhibits
- ☐ Generating Additional Revenue
- ☐ Other: _____

Finance
- ☐ Budgeting
- ☐ Cutting Expenses
- ☐ Other: _____

Benchmarking & Research
- ☐ Increasing Response Rate
- ☐ Other: _____

Membership
- ☐ Recruitment/Retention
- ☐ Communications
- ☐ Engagement
- ☐ Program Benefits
- ☐ Dues Structures
- ☐ Globalization
- ☐ Research
- ☐ Other: _____

Technology
- ☐ Other: _____

Time-Saving Tips
- ☐ Other: _____

Please submit your tip below. Please limit to 500 characters. If you require more than 500 characters, please submit via email directly to books@asaecenter.org with the subject "Tip".

_____

_____

_____

_____

_____

_____

_____

_____

_____

_____

_____

Continued on next page...

Share My Tip Form

continued from previous page

Name: _____

Organization: _____

_____

Email: _____

Please indicate whether you would like to remain anonymous or be credited as a tip contributor if your tip is published:

☐ Anonymous

☐ Yes, please list me as a contributor.

By submitting your tip, you represent and warrant that you are the sole author and proprietor of all rights in the work, that the work is original, that the work has not been previously published, that the work does not infringe any personal or property rights of another, that the work does not contain anything libelous or otherwise illegal, and that you have the authority to enter into this agreement and grant of license. You also agree that the work contains no material from other works protected by copyright that have been used without the written consent of the copyright owner and that ASAE & The Center for Association Leadership is under no obligation to publish your tip submission.

You also grant ASAE & The Center for Association Leadership the following rights: (1) to publish the work in all print, digital, and other known or unknown formats; (2) to reprint, make derivative works of, and otherwise reproduce the work in all print, digital, and other known or unknown formats; and (3) to grant limited sub-licenses to others for the right to reprint, make derivative works of, and otherwise reproduce the work in all print, digital, and other known or unknown formats.

Signature_____

Thank you for submitting your tip!